MW00831915

CRAFTING
A HAPPY LIFE

ALSO BY INDIA SUSANNE HOLDEN

The World Is Better Than You Think—
Developing an eye for the good around you

CRAFTING
A HAPPY LIFE

A Short-Read

INDIA SUSANNE HOLDEN

DivineSeed
Publishing

Published by *The DivineSeed* Publishing, Seattle, Washington
divineseed.org

Printed in the United States of America

Cover, exterior design, photo of India
and all other images by Emily Page
With editing by Melissa Scott

Cover image:
"Seite aus einem Poesiealbum von 1923"
By Xocolatl
License: GFDL (http://www.gnu.org/copyleft/fdl.html) or
CC-BY-SA-3.0 https://creativecommons.org/licenses/by-sa/3.0/
via Wikimedia Commons

1. Life Skills.   2. Personal Growth.   3. Happiness

ISBN-10:0-9970182-0-8
ISBN-13:978-0-9970182-0-2

First edition for print 2016

This is for you, my Angelman.
Love you bunches and bunches!

CONTENTS

CONTENTS

~ INTRODUCTION ~

Crafting a Happy Life is a small book, yet with big possibilities.

You can read it just to take a joyride along the river of life for a couple of hours. You can eat it up like a plateful of comfort food. (Mine is mashers and peas.)

You can also use it—whenever you see fit—as a guide and companion for crafting *your* happy life. With the ideas I've jotted down for you, such as being a rebel; eating dessert first; developing love as a tool—not just a feeling that comes over you; stealing pie; and loving "just because," you'll be on your way to a happy life in no time at all.

Many years ago, I healed myself from a time of depression. Along the way, I learned so much about what will and won't make me happy. Some of those things have helped other people, too. And I just love helping people.

I also have this huge passion for writing. So I thought I'd write us this journey along the river of life. I'm taking my raft down there right now. Want to come craft a happy life with me?

1

Out on the River

I've got a lump in my throat right now. It's caused by the thought that this may be it. That you and I, dear sweetheart, might finally get together, right here, on these pages.

You see, for over a decade, I've been *crafting a happy life* and I know, with what I'm going to show you in this handbook, so can you.

I will help you be happy like a *flippedy-floppedy*, laughing rainbow trout leaping from the water, chasing after dragonflies in the sunshine. Of course, this happiness will come at a price: Love. You will have to love yourself. Oh, the horror!

Still, you shouldn't have to struggle through these pages as if you were clumping laboriously along a muddy river bank after it rained. So I thought we'll make it an adventure. I'm thinking of Huckleberry Finn and his friend, Jim, going down the Mississippi River. We won't be catching fish, but we'll catch some ideas. We won't exactly look up at the slow drifting stars like Jim and Huck did at night, but we'll look at the stars that shine in our own hearts.

Where we make landfall, we'll slip into golden fields of understanding and friendship. We'll follow our noses and steal pie.

If that sounds good to you, then come on, hop on my raft. Look here, take this oar. You can pull it through the water like this. Off we go! And if we steer this thing aground, no worries, we'll jump into the water and push it free again. Let's be brave. I'll go first by confessing this: I can't ever seem to want to do *anything* like I'm supposed to. Not even writing—especially not writing. Because that's true, I've decided to take heart which means I won't edit this piece into the ground and never publish it at all. I promise to be honest instead of perfect. I might even break some writing rules. Yay! I already feel much encouraged! I love breaking rules!

So what do you think? Want to come along and be a scofflaw law with me? Take heart and defy convention? I hope so, because sticking your chin out at the rules sometimes is an essential ingredient of happiness.

What's that? You knew that? Great! Then thumb your nose at propriety even more! Unless you're holding out for gold stars if you're really good? Ah, what we won't do for those pointy-shaped bits of gold paper, right?

In Germany, where I went to school, instead of gold stars, we got little Victorian pictures sparkling with glitter. They were called *Poesiebildchen*. The best way I can translate that is as "little poetry pictures."

They were so cute, I could die! They showed things like little fluttery birds carrying ribbons and hearts in their beaks. Sometimes little fluffy lambs. Angels. Babies with kittens. Children in bloomers and lace-up boots. Considering the theme of our adventure—a journey on the river—I was tickled to find a poetry picture of a vessel on the water. It's not our raft, but it's just as romantic, what with the roses and an adorable little captain.

I loved those romantic depictions so much, I almost couldn't stand it. It's the same feeling I get when I watch baby animal videos.

To *craft a happy life*, letting the "cute" in is an important part. And it works, judging by the tens of millions of puppy and kitten videos and views.

True, those videos, as my *poetry pictures,* are kitschy, but that's what makes them so delightful! And your little heart longs for delight!

But it takes more than cuteness to make life happy. Something wild is needed, too: It requires a certain degree of comfort with the higgledy-piggledy, anarchic part of life, hence my suggestion that ignoring respectable society sometimes is part of happiness. As soon as you try too much to squelch chaos, life grows stale and hard around the edges like that last slice of bread left in the bag. You know—the dried-out bread end. The one you haven't thrown out, though you're already halfway into a new bag, because food should not be wasted. Well, toss it already. Be a rebel, in this and, of course, in other ways, too.

Besides opening up to life's cuteness and being a rebel, you can also play with the timeline of your life by rewriting your past. What? Really. Your subconscious won't know the difference because, as far as your brain is concerned, it all comes down to *experience*. Both, the things you vividly imagine, and things that actually happen, are recorded by your brain pretty much the same way. You can make up new stories for the parts of the past you don't like.

It seems nutty and you would think everybody did this if it worked. Mostly, people don't know it. But sports teams do, as an example. Some of them have been using vivid imagining—what they call "visualization"—for decades, turning their teams into winners. You've got to make it very vivid and repeat your better story of the past many times. But no more often than the painful memories you go over and over and over during your lifetime.

Of course, that's easier said than done as is true for much that is worthwhile. But if you apply yourself, you'll be surprised by how much of the past you can heal this way.

Then there's quantum theory. You can learn just enough about it to grossly abuse it and use it to make chaos your friend and to chuck past and future, as there apparently are none anyway, only an infinite *now*. The past, it appears, lives only in our memory and the future in our imagination. Quite glorious if you ask me. Perfect for mindfulness.

If you dare, go ahead; set yourself free from time's tyranny. Think you don't have time to be happy? Guess again. It takes seconds, if you know how. Looking at cute poetry pictures does it for me. A lot of people love videos of purring kitties, or goofy dogs, running into things. One of my favorites is a video of a dog getting a massage. You can tell it just loooves it and that makes me happy. With an internet connection, you can easily find something cute to look at that will tickle your funny bone and give you a boost of happy.

Another thing about *crafting happiness:* If you think you need to do that *thing* you need to do before you can do that other thing you *really* want to do, you are wrong. The river doesn't wait. It flows and flows and flows, constantly giving up chances to you. So don't wait. Do what you want to do now (if not all of it, then some of it). Eat dessert first! You might not live to the main course. I don't want to be indelicate, but people are dying while you are reading this. People who had a perfectly reasonable expectation to live through supper.

Let's be rebels and make our own adventures that are as unique as you and I are. If that suggestion gives you a little thrill, you probably *are* a rebel. Or want to be one. That's good. What could you do right now to defy your self-imposed limitations? Come to think of it, don't throw out that orphaned piece of bread hiding in the back of the refrigerator. Instead, stick it into the hearty broth of life and make it tasty again! Stop reading and do it. What silly, crazy thing could you do right now that would revive something in your life that's gone stale? How could you stir up just enough trouble right now to make this very moment delicious?

Why am I trying to egg you on like this? Because busting out of your routine feels good. It makes you happy. Isn't that what you want? If you don't, if you think you have to choose between a tasty life and a successful one (or whatever limiting ideas you've got around this), ask yourself if you have any proof that doing something *in order* to get something *else*, causes happiness, or success. Like, for example, making pots of money before following your bliss.

2

JUST BECAUSE

I'm glad you're still here. Even after I've rambled on about rebel rousing, little poetry pictures, eating dessert first, and floating on an imaginary river. Seems to me you really *are* interested in being happy. Are you? Please say yes. If you can't, that means we have a lot of extra work to do. I'd like to skip it. Can we go right to the "how" part? All right, I thought you might be up for it. Here it is: To be happy requires love. That again? Yup. No love. No happy.

Are you saying, "Duh?" right now?

Ha! I don't mean romantic love. Romantic love is what everybody under thirty thinks will make them plain delirious with happiness—hence all that furious mating. No, romantic love isn't it. And worse, because it isn't "it," when we find our mate but not happiness, some of us (e.g., me) become cynical about love and romance and start looking in all the wrong places—like money and prestige, or a good party—for that elusive something that brings us happiness.

The love I'm talking about is the kind without qualifiers. That's what brings lasting happiness. Do you already see how practicing gratitude is a path to unqualified love? If you're pondering it, that's good. Don't worry, it'll come. I once wrote a manuscript of fifty-four chapters to describe how wonderful we actually are before I noticed that not one of them was about love. It's not that I was too dumb to get it. But I was so steeped in love, I didn't notice how much of a starring role it played in making us so wonderful. Sort of like a fish not knowing it's swimming in water. So, it may not be obvious, but to *craft a happy life* takes love. Specifically, love without qualifiers, commonly known as unconditional love. Which means "love just because."

You know how when you ask kids a goofy grown-up question about why they are doing something and they look at you like you're weird and they give you a long drawn out, "Becaaause"? That's what I mean: Love without qualifiers is "love, becaaause."

Crafting a happy life is a lot about that. You don't do it by reframing your reality to change your perspective. You don't do it by focusing your mind on your goals, or meditating, or using your imagination. You don't do it by getting out into nature and your hands into the dirt. These are all just your basic necessary tools and conditions for having a good life in general. But none of that means anything without love, particularly love "just because." And that's where you're screwed right now. Because that's not in your repertoire.

"Huh?" you say. "It is, too!"

It's not. Undoubtedly you love somebody—a darling spouse, kids, a loyal dog, a fluffy cat, lounging on the back of your sofa. Of course, you love lots of things, people, places, ideas, and memories. But that's very different from having unconditional love in your repertoire. So what the heck is that supposed to mean?

Repertoire, according to the dictionary, means "the entire stock of skills, techniques, devices, or tools used in a particular field." We're talking about love like a "field of expertise", not just like a feeling. In a happy life, love is the practice of the entire "stock of skills," such as acceptance, gratitude, presence, and thankfulness.

When you look upon it like this, love is a device. A device that heals. It is a technique. A technique of understanding and of listening. It is a tool. A tool of celebrating and honoring. That's the kind of love anyone who wants to be happy needs to have in their repertoire. With some practice, it can be in yours.

A quick way to use love like a tool for *crafting a happy life* is to adopt this simple motto: "How can I apply love here?" For example, your sibling (we won't name names) annoys the bejesus out of you with their unsolicited advice. Instead of rolling your eyes, what you think is, "How can I apply love here?" Now, this isn't about letting that person off the hook when they behave badly, or being passive, or always turning the other cheek. This is about happiness. Getting all worked up about your sibling puts a stink on that. (All right, yeah, I'm talking about my own life.)

So, instead of thinking, "What a ding-dong," I'm thinking, "How can I apply love here?" Instead of arguing, I say, "Thank you for the advice." Do I mean it? No, I do not. Would I rather love my relative than school them when that schooling is proven not to work? Yes I do! I think that's a better choice.

Use your judgment. Sometimes you have to say, "Step off!" Sometimes you apply love to the situation. If the net outcome is happiness, then you've got a good balance.

As the motto, "How can I *apply* love here," implies, I am not talking about the kind of love that "comes over you" as Eric Clapton croons in his sweet song "Running on Faith." I'm writing about the kind of love that comes from within. You produce it naturally like milk from your breast, like ambrosia from the heart of plenty. You are overflowing with it like a brimming river glittering in the sunlight. Really. The proof's in the puddin', so, for now, just go with it. The proof will follow.

Right now, if your raft lies pulled up on shore and you're sitting there brooding over the crappy way of things, I trust your feelings are justified. But look at that river! The water twinkling in the sunlight! Look down the river; see how it disappears around the bend? You want to know what's behind there, don't you?

Now's a good time to explore. Put some spit in your hands, drag that raft back into the water. Hop on! Grab your oar and let's go!

Oh my goodness! Look at how the heavens are opening up! It's pouring buckets just when we get going! Wasn't the sun shining just a second ago? It still is. Right on the other side of those black clouds.

It's okay, keep your oar going. The rain'll stop or we'll paddle right out of it! And the sheer fact is, even when it's raining here, somewhere the sun is shining. Whether on little birds rising with a song or on little feathered heads, nodding off in little nests, beaks tucked under little wings—just like in the poetry pictures of my childhood. In the same way the sun is always going, happiness is always in the air, ready for you to snatch it to your heart.

As you read this, think about the magic of life. See if you can't let it in a little. Like sunshine, it's always there, waiting to be remembered. Life's treasures are as shiny as a gold star, as glimmery as Victorian poetry pictures, practically encrusted with the most sparkly, sparkle dust.

Sure, we can expect rocks and boulders in the river, and sandbars, here and there. Maybe even rapids and falls. But if we keep going, we'll get to the river's mouth and paddle right into the great shiny sea of love.

3

HOLTY POLTY
ROCK YOUR BOAT

"One must still have chaos within oneself,
to give birth to a dancing star."
– Friedrich Nietzsche, *Thus Spake Zarathustra*

You know now why I loved those pretty little poetry pictures, don't you? It's because they incited love in me. What incites love in you? The first thing that just came to your mind—go with that. No kidding. You won't come up with anything better. That first thought was the truth. If you thought nothing, then you did a lightning-fast and automatic edit before you could catch that little slippery fish of a hopeful impulse.

Speaking of hope, do you secretly believe that what would make you happy is out of reach for you? Well, if that's true, we've got to do something about it because that would be the end of the story, right there. And what a loss that would be! Because everybody has something that brings out the love. Knowing what it is for you will help you craft a happy life.

But listen, don't stress yourself. We're just getting rolling. Remember that we're on an adventure! Adventures go holty-polty—riding your raft on the river of life, water sprays in your face, fish jump, people wave from shore as you glide by. All is never lost, as well as all is never won. That's as it should be—life is dynamic! Your raft rides up the waves, your raft rides down the waves. You catch the rhythm of it as soon as you make room for the holty-polty of life. You wipe the water from your eyes and see again. You dry out. Better than new because you made it through.

You're out in the open now, not in a polite

wood-paneled office somewhere, lying on a couch, one hand resting heroically against your forehead. You can be wildly honest, here. I have every confidence that, deep down, you know what will bestir your heart even if you don't know yet what that is. Trust me, it'll come.

And if some idea about what will incite love in you sprang forth in the last thirty seconds, go with that. Just go! Give that to yourself. Zarathustra has nothing on you; you can birth your own dancing star! Whether it's being an aerialist, winding yourself up in bright red silks, bathing puppies at an animal shelter, singing at the top of your lungs to your favorite heavy metal tracks from high school, taking a free online course in higher mathematics, or renting a fast car. Whether it's just for you or someone else—have at it. If it lets you feel the love, you know you've hit on one of the tributaries that lead to a happy life.

Or if you're just not sure, don't torture yourself! Instead, try for something you think is really out there beyond your comfort zone. That'll be sure to rock the status quo and lead you to who knows what—maybe the thing that's just right for you!

If you're ready to explore, I have a few suggestions, for starters. And I hope you're ready. Because the difference between reading and acting is as big as the difference between a dream and reality. Until now, this is only an imaginary river, a fantasy raft, and a mirage of an ocean of love. But that can change. The love can become real if you're willing to act.

Build that stock of skills so you can add love into your repertoire. The quickest way to prime your love is to work up a nice froth of gratitude. It's a decision as simple as getting up and making a cup of coffee. You ponder it. You decide it. You get up. You do it. Gratitude is a feeling of loving appreciation. Such as you have for the nutty, chocolatey aroma of coffee or the subtle fragrance of your Earl Grey when you hold the bag under your nose and give it a little squeeze.

You ponder it.

"Should I look right now for something to be

grateful for?"

You decide it.

"Why yes, my dear, I believe I shall!"

You do it.

"Ah, giving this body a stretch, reaching for the toes, feels so yummy."

A stretch is a small thing. That's how it should be at the start. When practicing gratitude, come at it with a mindset of entering the world out the humble kitchen door where you can inhale the sweet air, purvey your domain, and get good and grounded, rather than the grand foyer where you're distracted by the idea of red carpets, flashbulbs strobing in the night like fireworks, and paparazzi shouting your name. Followed up the next morning by a write-up of your feats of gratitude. That's just too much pressure!

You want to build your skills gradually. In the beginning, set modest goals. That way, you don't overreach, setting yourself up for a fall.

Also, the less significant the things you choose to be grateful for, the easier they are to come by.

Let's see. What can you appreciate?

TAKE A LOOK AT THIS STARTER LIST

The soft blanket that covers you at night.

The switch that turns the light on instantly

The minty taste of your toothpaste

Well-fitting shoes

A swept-clean sidewalk

To grow your own list you can get a good start by asking: "What can I be more grateful for?" Then cast about for things right around you and fan out from there. The more concrete, the better, such as how good it feels to wash your hands in warm water on a wintry day, or feel the warmth of the sun on your closed eye lids. Sensations are easier to appreciate than concepts like having good health.

At this point, let me caution you not to fall to the idea that you're practicing gratitude because you're not thankful enough. I suggest practicing love in the form of gratitude so you can turn love into a skill and because every time you give a nod to something good in your life, you change the neural networks in your brain, building a brain that more readily recognizes the good around you and more easily feels appreciation for it, priming you for that loving feeling.

A word about your nature and how it will affect your success. If you're the kind of individual who wants to do some paddling—but not too much—before you pull up on shore for a rest, that's good to know. It just means that you ought to give yourself a little longer before you see big changes in your mind's scenery.

Albert Einstein famously said, "Problems cannot be solved with the same mindset that created them," in other words, things change when the mind that created them changes.

Here is why Einstein's insight is so useful:

As we've learned from the field of neuroscience, the neural networks in your brain are like sticks of silly putty—shapeable! They're shaped by what you do!

This means that when you rock your boat and try something new, rather than drown or get in trouble (well, you might a little) you'll create a new mind, i.e., a new mindset. If you shape it just right, it's no longer circumstances that decide how you feel, *you* do! Your activities and sensations, thinking and feeling, change your brain. If you're strategic, you can turn yourself into someone who loves whatever, whenever you choose to love, just because. And that, sweetheart, is a superpower you can use to *craft a happy life.*

On the river of your life, there are big fat cruise ships you have to navigate around, and cargo barges to stay out of the way of so they don't ram and drown you. There are speedboats racing by, and rowboats cleaving close to shore. You can shout,

"Hello," and invite them to tie to your raft and come aboard for a cookout.

And then there are the rafts just like yours. You salute each other. Sometimes you have dance parties at night by lantern light.

Life is gritty, yet tasty—like a piece of pie you picked up after it fell to the ground. But its natural sweetness makes it worth eating it all up. How do I know with such certainty that this is so? Because I have faced death three times along my journey, and each time that is what I found.

Each time I believed it's over, I got stunned by how, looking back, though life was a topsy-turvy adventure, each moment was too precious for words anyway. This is not true for everyone. And that's something that deserves respect. Though, seeing as you're still hanging around these pages, I suspect you're one of those with a strong longing to taste the happy sweetness, never mind the grit.

In the next chapter, I'll say more about just how to practice reaching out for the pie.

What's your favorite? Cherry? Rhubarb? Apricot? Blueberry? Pecan? Oh?! Is it apple?

.

4

PIE THIEF

You just might need to be a little crafty and brave because you may have to steal pie off a windowsill like Huck Finn did with pounding heart, on his adventure with Jim.

Remember in the beginning when I wrote about being brave, admitting that I can't follow the rules to save my life? It's your turn to be brave by looking at what *you* can't or won't do. Be brave and ask yourself, "What's poking me in the side? What's trying to get my attention?"

Something always has to be overcome, some risk taken—that's the price. My price was to write this guide for us. More than a few drafts, more than a few months, more than a few doubts. I've never written like this before—easygoing. This time, I resisted trying to impress. If this book speaks to you, you won't need convincing, if it doesn't, could I turn you around with research studies and fancy footwork? I doubt it. And I'm having so much more fun doing it like this: writing from my heart instead of from the urge to demonstrate my credibility. Doing this, writing and trusting in my writing, makes me feel so good because writing is how I *craft my happy life* right now.

What do you doubt? What is asking for your trust? What can you start doing right now to *craft your happy life*? If the answer is murky, that's okay. You're not dead in the water. The currents of your desire can carry both, you *and* your doubts forward, if you let them.

But you also need provisions. To get your satchel full of what you need, you may have to steal some things—like pie—because life might not be forthcoming with all that will nourish you and build you up. Being a pie thief—to give yourself what life won't—takes a lot of bravery. In some odd, funny little way, we give ourselves what others indicate we deserve. I say phooey! I'm not in the mood for wheedling, or bartering, or waiting, and I'm certainly not doing without! What the world won't provide, I'll find a way to give to myself. And so can you!

Eating pie, being a rebel, letting yourself have some, or all, of what you really want, busting out of your routines and embracing the holty-polty of this ride—all of it helps you unmoor your raft and give you the oomph and strength to join this life.

So does unqualified love.

Those things change your brain and make you so much better at filling your cup with the sweet milk of life. Pie is so good with milk.

But we've also got to make sure that your cup doesn't have too many cracks in it so you can hold on to what you scoop up. To make your cup whole, we've got to see to it that *you* are whole. Otherwise, the joy keeps seeping out. The little milk left over turns sour. The pie crust gets hard. Oh, no!

To be whole, you need a really good friendship

with yourself. But never fear! You're already learning the best possible way to become your own sweetheart and fill any cracks: The tool of unqualified love directed toward yourself.

TWO THINGS OF NOTE HERE:

For one, if you already love yourself like a champ, you can create more wholeness (and change your brain) by extending that love outward toward the world. Conversely, if you already love the world, warts 'n all, mind you, then you can extend that love to yourself. Unqualified love works, no matter what direction you aim it in.

Secondly, if it's trust you're missing (like I did), or faith in yourself or in the world, then just switch "love" out with "trust." Or hope, or confidence. Really, with whatever you want more and better of.

This works because you can turn any feeling— whether it's love, trust, confidence, etc.,—from an emotional response that happens *to* you into a skill you can wield by building out your brain with new neural networks and creating your own triggers to activate them (like pretty poetry pictures, cute animal videos, objects of gratitude, being a rebel, and so forth). But I want to say that, regardless of what you want to build out, if you do not have the love down yet, then start there because love is the foundation, even for trust, even for hope, even for confidence.

You cannot succeed with an enemy where there should be a helping friend, and if you don't feel the love for yourself, then you're not a very good friend to yourself. If you don't feel it for the world, then the world is not your friend and you're on your own, instead of being free to ask for its support.

To become a great friend to your own self, praise yourself generously because praise incites love.

You know how, when someone compliments you on your shirt or says, "Good job!" you right away like them better? We love getting praised. So praise yourself without shame! I guarantee you, you'll like it (after you get over the weirdness). Did you make your bed? Did you floss? Did you feed the dog? The cat? The neighborhood squirrels and crows? Did you start work on time? Did you remember to pick up the thingy? Did you remember to eat a fruit today? A vegetable? Did you patiently listen to your friend tell the same story, again? All praise-worthy. As I said earlier, start small.

It's only natural if you feel some resistance. Praise is supposed to come from other places, we're told, not out of our own mouths. You know by now, don't you, that I'm not talking about being a braggart. I'm talking about being honest-to-goodness good to yourself. I'm talking about not waiting until the world deigns to treat you right and build you up.

Imagine it's Sunday. The sun is out. It's just a little before noon. The world's set out its pies on the window sills. Smells so good.

Go get yourself some.

Do I mean you should become a thief? Of course not. *Of course, you bake your own pie.* But the thing is that we humans are funny: we think that pie (in this instance, pie stands for praise) is baked by others and we can only watch from afar until we get lucky and someone cuts us a piece. So, praising ourselves *feels* questionable, even downright illegitimate! To sidestep the weirdness, think of being a pie thief as being a gentleman robber—it's for a good cause: a loving friendship with yourself.

Handy-Dandy List No.1

1. Break some rules
2. Eat dessert first
3. Love just because
4. Give yourself that thing you love
5. Change how you remember the past so it suits you better
6. Allow for some chaos by busting up a routine
7. Develop love as a tool through a <u>daily</u> practice of gratitude
8. Rock your boat on purpose

A Fine Shady Place
for Sweet-Talking

So far, we've built up mental understanding. Now we have to build up physical understanding, by creating visceral experiences you can feel in your gut. As I wrote earlier, reading about how to *craft a happy* life isn't enough. Likewise, understanding in your *head* about unqualified love won't make you feel it.

That would be like writing in a love letter, "Oh, feel my lips on your lips. They're so soft and warm and…"

Whole bookshelves are filled with such delicious writing. But no one in their right mind would ever think that's as good as a real smooch from your sweetheart.

To build a bridge from imagining your happiness to feeling it all over, I gave you the list of eight things you can do right now. I assure you, if you mix them into your everyday life, they work. The more you dare to break some rules, eat dessert first—meaning reward yourself—just because you can, and not because you've, "earned" it, the closer you feel to yourself. This is not to say that you should be glutinous. Use your discernment: What makes you feel like a co-conspirator? Like you're in league with yourself with the goal of *crafting a happy life*? The more you let yourself have some of your heart's secret desires—and all the rest—the quicker your loving friendship with yourself advances.

There is another thing I want you to add to your list of things to practice. It's the trickiest of the bunch and, thus, requires even more craftiness. Partially because you might really feel stupid doing it. You'll just have to outwit your own embarrassment. But, trust me, it'll be worth it, so let's get cracking.

If I were to tell you to practice saying something beautiful about the world, do you think you could do it?

Could you say something like, "Amazon forest, you're so green and lush. And, on top of that, you provide this world with so much oxygen! How amazing is that? Thank you!"?

That's sweet-talking. It's a wonderful balm for when life puts a blister on you. Stop for a minute and try it out.

Now, let's step it up and move a little closer to home. Say something like, "I appreciate you teachers who come to school every morning, teaching your hearts out."

For this to work, you need to actually say those, or similarly complementary words. Just do it, and then we'll talk about it. Nope! Do not read ahead. To keep it simple, you can just read the two praising sentences aloud. Get into it with real feeling, sweetheart. Uhn, uhn, uhn. Do not turn that page!

Did you do it? Was it awkward? If it was, I hope you also noticed that something about it felt nice.

Sweet-talking has in common with the practice of gratitude that it is *appreciative*. But there's an important difference that makes them both equally necessary to *crafting a happy life:* You practice gratitude to help turn love into a skill. You practice sweet-talking—once directed toward yourself, which is next—to turn you into your own best friend. The very thing we started to talk about in the last chapter.

Sweet-talking yourself gives you a real-life experience of being treated with love and kindness. This is not just a psychological event, though it is that. It's also *physical*. If you remember, you read about this at the beginning of this book: Your subconscious responds the same, whether something happens "out there" in the world or you vividly imagine it. Same with whether someone else treats you sweetly or if you're the one doing it. Feeling loved, no matter the source, increases your levels of *oxytocin*—the bonding hormone. So when you are sweet to yourself, it makes you bond more with yourself.

Because, at first, this feels a little odd, I had you start by practicing it on the world. Now it's time to practice on darling you.

Let's pull ashore over there in that fine shady place. Here, have some bread and cheese, and a slice of apple to fortify you. Oh, I brought some gold stars along in my knapsack, too.

To prove my point that what you think and say affects you and that sweet-talking will help you *craft a happy life*, I want you to practice on yourself now.

It works even better when you add patting yourself in a soothing way, like your shoulder or your arm, or on the head.

Feeling awkward? Understandable.

I know you can do this. And if you can't think of anything to say, use this:

"Sweetheart, you are awesome. I love how you always keep growing and learning. I love you so much!"

This *does* take some courage. You already

39

practiced saying something nice about the world (The Amazon forest) and about other people (the teachers). This is just the next step. If it's easier to say something beautiful about other people than about yourself, well, to someone else, *you're* "other people." Think about that.

If you don't want to do it, I'm sorry to say, the demonstration won't work. So give it a try. Say those words like a real sweet-talker; put your heart into it.

"Hello my love. I'm so proud of you. You're a beautiful person. And I'm so happy to be with you."

Don't forget to give yourself a pat on the shoulder or place your hand on your heart; that's a good one, too. At first, it seems a little weird, but it works and it's just the two of us, and I can't see you do it, so don't be too embarrassed.

Okay. I am going to assume you've done it. If you haven't, I don't see the point in your reading on. Basically, what I'm saying here is that, if you don't help steer the raft, there's no getting down the river. And I so want us to finish our journey. I'm just dying to share my gold stars. So, give yourself a push and repeat after me.

"Sweetheart, you're the best! I love you so much for working so hard on making a good life and being happy."

You did it!! You're awesome! Good job! Yay!! Here is your gold star! Take two. Stick 'em one on each earlobe like earrings. Aww, you're beautiful, like a basket full of fresh-picked peaches. You're right as rain. Cuter than a...okay, I'll stop now.

How do you feel now? If you sweet-talked yourself like the deserving sweetie you really are, you should have perked up a bit. If not, please do try again.

Like I said, it takes some courage. Just try again. Go along this grassy shore some ways. I'll be right here when you come back. Sit with yourself. Say something nice. If it helps, imagine saying it first to someone else you really like. No, it's not silly at all. It's a darling thing to do.

It's so important because, once you can see for yourself that what you say has an effect, you can put it to use with glee! By treating yourself right—and especially by sweet-talking yourself—you can become the best friend you've ever had. It works even better if you haven't done a thing to "deserve" it because you show yourself that you always deserve your love. Nothing you need to do or be for that to be true. That's genuine unqualified love.

This love starts right where you are. Now's the time. Not later, after you've read this book or accidentally stuffed it down the garbage disposal because I won't shut up!

To be fair—I admit it—sweet-talking to yourself is one of the harder practices. I didn't tell you right away because I forgot. Loving myself unconditionally has become so normal, I forgot about all the time I spent practicing it, and still do.

Sure, we're told not to toot our own horns, self-praise stinks, don't be full of yourself, don't be arrogant. But none of that is what we're doing here. We're being healthy! And being honestly good to yourself is what you deserve as much as anyone else you love.

Sweetheart, to succeed at *crafting a happy life*, part of that is being willing to find true love for yourself.

From experience, I can tell you, this practice will become natural like you've always done it. And because praise incites love, getting praise from yourself will make you love *you* more. Having such a champion in yourself will increase your self-confidence and fill you with a warm fellow feeling towards yourself.

Everything starts with you, right where you are. So, love yourself like you're a stack of delicious hotcakes fresh off the griddle with melted butter and a sprinkling of cinnamon! Practice that sweet-talking!

Every little thing that ever happened to you, whether someone else did it to you or you did it to yourself, is represented in your brain. That's real science. If we were to look inside your brain right now, we'd see neural networks built by, among other things, the self-talk that is critical of you. If you're more often rude to yourself than nice, you have more rude-associated structures in your brain. With your new sweet-talking (which you are starting now, right?), you're adding a bunch of new structures, literally creating a brain full of happiness-associated neural networks. That's the kind of brain that can *craft a happy life*! So say it again and again:

"Hello darling. I love you. You are wonderful and beautiful and I'm so happy to be with you. Thank you for being with me and for being such a good sport."

Praise yourself at every turn, every hour. Incite that loving feeling.

By the time you're finished reading these pages, I want you to have a solid start at sweet-talking. Like I said earlier, this is not love as a feeling that comes over you, but love as a choice you intentionally make, like getting up and making coffee. The more you do it, the better you feel. The better you feel, the more you do it until there's so much love in you, it sloshes over the rim of your heart and splashes out onto other people, bigger than a drive-by in the rain. That's when things gets really, really good because wherever you go, there's a better than good chance that love will be incited and the world made better than it already is.

For example, I just made a call to a shop that sells window blinds to find a replacement end cap. They blew me off.

"You need to contact the company that installed your blinds."

I'm renting, I don't know who did it. Right then, for such a small thing, I could have become annoyed. So often it's the small insignificant things that do it to us. Instead, I kept my cool.

I told myself, "You're so awesome, making that call. I love your tenacity! I bet you can make another. I know you will!"

Two more calls. Same answer both times. Still cool. Getting even more proud of myself for the sheer fact that I'm persevering. The fourth call was the charm.

"No problem, I can help you. What's your address? How many do you need? Done, expect them in the mail."

"How much?" I asked. "Absolutely free," she said.

Wow! That, too, is a small thing. But sweet-talking myself instead of getting my boxers (yes, 100% plaid cotton boxers) in a twist on the other calls, I can really revel in this small kindness now. It's a good day!

Sweet-talking yourself helps turn you into your own greatest ally—when someone blows you off, you're not on your own. People may ignore you, but there you are, fortifying *you*. Sure, you have other allies, but not as conveniently nearby.

Also, if you're not an ally to yourself, you have to ask, what are you?

So sweet-talk yourself, like every day! Build a loving mind because a loving mind builds *you* up, grows your confidence and trust, and makes love present, right where you stand. This awesome, loving brain sees the world so differently from how you used to see it!

It notices goodness all around. The beautiful trees that grow along the street you take to the store.

Piles of dark clouds and a golden fan of sunshine that comes through a break.

That self-loving brain is more relaxed and, thus, more forgiving of the foibles and failures of others. Instead of clamping your teeth together, you just shrug (and maybe roll your eyes just a little).

Like tourists finding the beach, like kids remembering the way to the ice cream parlor, a loving brain is drawn to manifestations of love, joy, and humanity, in news programs, at the office, at the grocery store, and even in the parking lot of said grocery store. Your loving brain finds reasons for empathy and compassion for strangers and your family, alike. And it has a perfectly valid reason: "Bccaaause."

I am going to make the assumption that, having read all this, you feel kind of good. That's the plan, anyway. This's been fun, right? Okay, so, before I set down the final end period of this chapter, I want you to do the other part of this exercise so I can prove to you that sweet-talking works. This time by having you do the opposite! Instead of saying something lovely, say something crappy.

Here is an example:

"This is all poppycock. I can't 'craft a happy life' with a bunch of softheaded ideas."

You can even add air quotations.

Say it in earnest like you mean it. You can handle this.

"I don't know why I bothered reading this idiotic book! I don't have control over how other people make me feel!"

Now, did that change how you feel? Not quite as pleasant as before? If it changed how you feel, then you know this process is real, that what you tell yourself makes a difference in how you feel. Then you know that the happy talk and self-love have an effect, just like mean talk does. Remember that.

So, how can you fix the crappy feeling you just induced? Exactly! You got it! With sweet-talk.

Like this: "I was just kidding. An experiment. This works. I love you. There, there, it'll all be okay. We can craft this happy life. It's easy. Good job! I'm really proud of you!"

6

JUGGLERS IN THE TOWN SQUARE

Now that you know how much of an effect what you say has, let's give some thought to the habit of fretting and surmising.

Fretting: "What if they don't make my end caps anymore?"

Surmising: "That woman on the phone didn't care one whit about me needing those end caps."

Are you saying, "That's just harmless grousing. No big deal"? I hear you. You're right, it's not. And it is. I will demonstrate the truth of that. The idle chatter in our heads really doesn't mean much. La-la-la. "Hey, where is the barista?

I've been waiting for two whole minutes!" La-la-la. "Look at the couple sitting over there not even talking to each other—how sad is that." La-la-la. "Ugh! Rain forecast for the whole weeek." La-la-la.

Like I said, I agree, it doesn't mean much. But that doesn't mean that it doesn't have an effect. See? Not meaning anything is not synonymous with not having an effect.

What your brain is thinking does make an impact. Case in point: The sweet and crappy talk we just went over in the last chapter.

And here's the kicker. Fretting has even *more* of an effect than sweet-talking: Our brains are veritable sponges for negativity the better to avoid being eaten by an alligator or a mountain lion. If your ancestor couldn't find that blackberry patch again—oh, darn. But if they didn't pay attention and remember where the alligators congregate? Good eats! For the gators.

I agree with you one hundred percent if you're thinking, "I'll neither be able, nor am I willing, to quit fretting and surmising and complaining."

And you shouldn't. We still have some big critters to watch out for.

Here is where the eighth tool, *juggling*, comes in. With not one, but multiple balls. Because, after all, one ball is not juggling. Imagine dark blues and greens, magentas, deep purples for things like moaning and groaning, and fretting and getting angry, or afraid. Think of yellow balls and orange and pink and gold and silver for sweet-talking, eating dessert first, gratitude, pie, and unqualified love.

Imagine Huck and Jim seeing all the lights on in a town they pass at night. They paddle hard to get to shore just down from that place. After they've hidden the raft in the cattails, they sneak back, right into the town square. People are laughing and festivalling, oohing and aahing. Jugglers are juggling balls of many different colors, higher and higher. They keep them all mixed together, creating a dazzling display! The brighter balls catch the light more than the darker balls. But all of them together, make the show beautiful.

Juggling all different kinds of thoughts and feelings, you can let them exist side by side. But you can be mindful of what they do and don't do. The bright thoughts and feelings catch the light of joy, the darker ones give depth. Both are needed for a well-rounded life.

So you see, it's not about never yelling at yourself and praising yourself exclusively. It's about being strategic: What mix makes the best show? What *crafts the happiest life* for you?

7

LOVING THE RIVER

Imagine Jim and Huck, how excitedly they would talk on the way back down to where they hid the raft.

"So many balls at the same time!"

"And the one fella made them fly so high!"

"Holy moly! Did you see that?!"

"Yup. I did see."

"That was the best!"

It would surely be a moment of unqualified enjoyment.

That's the magic. Because if the love for the moment needs nothing to qualify it, nothing can stop it from happening. If, in our lives, nothing is required for us to love the moment, except our decision to choose to wield love like a tool instead of a feeling that comes over us, nothing can keep it down.

Then, we don't need the right kind of family; the right kind of pay; the right kind of kids, spouses, jobs, mornings, noons, and nights. Then, we don't need the stars to align before we can be happy.

Life offers us so many goodies if we don't sweat the details too, too much.

For example, the end caps for my blinds that came in the mail didn't fit. Apparently no one makes that part anymore. And, guess what, we found out the shades work without them.

The French have a great saying, c*omme ci, comme ça* (pron. comsi comsa), meaning "like this, like that." And that about sums up my point—you can love the river like it is. You can love life the same way—no qualifiers needed.

And when you do, love can operate reliably, and independent of circumstances. Free like a river's waters from the shore, untethered like a raft, able to flow on that big ol' river of your life. If life doesn't have to meet too many conditions or demands, it's like a river without a dam—flowing free with much less to gum things up.

As you practice your juggling, enjoying all the hues of life for the colorful show they, together, put on, *crafting a happy life* is hardly any work at all: You front-load the effort by creating a receptive mind that is crafty enough to see something of intrigue where before it saw something unwanted. And suddenly, there's so much good to delight over, you can hardly keep up.

8

NEW ADVENTURES

I'm proud of you! This is a small book, but small doesn't mean easy. I bet you feel challenged. I *hope* you feel challenged! And encouraged!

What with stealing pie and cultivating yourself as the best friend you ever had.

Be brave. Challenge reality as it appears now. Stick your chin out. Get your own supply of gold stars.

Let cute things tickle you.

You can practice all sorts of things that change your heart and mind into the kind that can *craft a happy life*. The more ordinary, the easier they're to come by. Like being grateful for your mittens; for a dirty penny on the street; a mumbled, "Have a nice day."

A dash of cayenne pepper in your smoothie makes it taste different in a good way. A lemon slice dipped into sugar is so good, my mouth waters, just writing it down. Have a snuggly blanket handy when it's cold outside. In the summer, put sandals in your bag and set your feet free when you leave work. If you need soothing, pet yourself as gently as a loving mom.

You can take advantage of the fact that you can reshape your brain by turning sweet-talking yourself into the best assets that won't see a resume (or will it?).

You can use the marvelous malleability of your brain to make new memories by vividly imagining how you *wish* it'd happened.

Quantum theory is calling. You can do a little research to help you rethink chaos and trouble as different-colored "balls."

Listen into your innermost self with the affection of a bestie. What does your heart really want? Trust that. Give yourself some, or all, of that, now! If you can't say for certain, then do something whacky or different—goad a new adventure into your life!

You are an exquisite human being. Deserving of everything good. So, go ahead and lick that plate!

Be like the little children and love just becaaause. Remember, love is not just a feeling that comes over you. You can turn it into a tool by practicing gratitude, daily, and doing anything else that incites love in you.

Write "How can I apply love here?" on a little slip of paper and stick it to the frame of your TV.

Follow the river around the bend to see what's there. Rock your raft on purpose and laugh, showing all your teeth. If you feel like crying instead, let yourself. Laughing and crying are your body's natural ways to release.

Remember that, though life is very gritty, its natural sweetness makes it worth gobbling up.

And remember, pie is good with milk.

Praise is good for your soul, so praise yourself with ardor, and do it so often that you fall in love—with you.

If you keep going to overflowing, you can give away the surplus of your unqualified love to any bystander, innocent or otherwise, just because; no deservingness required. Thus you make a good world better.

If you keep it up—with the neural networks you're building—you're going to have such a different experience of yourself, your life, and the world around you than you've had in the past. By giving yourself unqualified love, you make yourself happy, going through the rest of your life with a forever friend: You.

It took this long to build the brain you have now. So give it time. Love. Raft. Rest. Explore. Sweet-talk. Sneak pie. Spit the gravel into the grass, like it was seeds.

While writing this guide to *crafting a happy life*,

memories of the story of Huckleberry Finn and his intrepid friend, Jim kept me company. How they formed a bond of love even when the world disapproved—the kind of bond you can form with yourself, even when the world gives you a frown. It wasn't a perfect story, given how it was influenced by the times in which it was told. Still, these two buddies overcame all kinds of obstacles with their craftiness and the heart they put into doing so.

You can be crafty too and work around your limitations and the limitations of this time. When you float on the river and the moonlight lays a path across the water, notice how the ripples you create with your oar change that path. *You* did that!

And you're not alone. Re-read these pages often and I'll be your companion on the river. We'll watch fireflies glimmer on a warm summer night.

Your love light shines as beautiful.

For the Handy-Dandy Recap List, see the next page.

Handy-Dandy List No. 2

1. Steal pie. It's gritty *and* sweet
2. Praise, praise, praise
3. Sweet-talk
4. Let yourself fall in love with you
5. Pet yourself—don't be nervous
6. Love the river like it is
7. Rock your raft
8. Juggle with balls of every color-together!
9. Court new adventures

WHY I WROTE
CRAFTING A HAPPY LIFE

A hundred different things combined to make me write this thing. For example, the mystical experiences that are so precious to me and make my life so beautiful that I could never muster enough awe and gratitude to do them justice. They make me feel the amazing presence of the divine all around me and within me.

But I didn't always feel it. For a few years, in the early 90's, during the first U.S. invasion of Iraq, I suffered from depression. I didn't know it because I laughed all the time. But my body felt sluggish and achy. To see where I was going while backing up the car, I had to twist my whole upper body because my neck was so stiff. My hands felt kind of numb most of the time. I got worried that I might be really sick or something. So I went to see a friend's doctor, Dr. Ramesh Patel. He grilled me with a ton of questions. "Are you depressed," he finally asked me, point blank.

"No, not at all! I love to laugh and get excited about the day!" I said. All of a sudden, my cheeks kind of shook. I felt my lips tremble. Was I going to cry? Why? Later, while walking me to the door, the doc put his arm around my shoulders and said, "You're either an alcoholic, or you're depressed. We'll see." When I came back the next week, he pointed at my test results and said, "You told the truth, you're not an alcoholic." He prescribed some things for me to take. Being a rebel, instead of the pharmacy, I went straight to the library and read up on depression. Some of the descriptions felt like someone had been following me around, taking notes. Down to the swollen lymph nodes and numb-but-tingling hands.

Later, I stood in the shower. I noticed that I was moping and mulling. It came to me that I'd been grieving ever since the war against Iraq began. But it was over. I said loudly, "Stop." Right then, I committed to being happy again. I listened to what my soul was saying to me and made changes. I still do, because I'm never done evolving.

I visited Dr. Patel one other time to see what he

thought about me changing my life around rather than taking medication to lift the depression. Seeing how much better I was doing already, he agreed—for the time being—if I kept improving. Though it had lasted for several years, it seemed my depression was what they call "situational" (because of the war) rather than "clinical." Meaning that by changing the situation (realizing the war was over), I could get better.

I just hadn't caught on to the emotional hole I was in. Once I saw it, I was able to make the changes that helped me heal. (As a quick aside, one of the big changes I made was to stop being fake-nice for social purposes. I didn't even say, "I'm fine," if I wasn't. I may eventually write a Short-Read about that experience.)

I don't want to beat a dead horse here, but I feel it's necessary to mention that I don't, in any way, advocate for people not to take the medicines they and their doctors decide will be helpful to them. Being a rebel, I *do* advocate for you, sweetheart. Listen to the doc *and* listen to the divine voice inside you, if you can. See if you can let it guide you, *in addition* to your doc's suggestions. It always takes two—you *and* the doc. A doctor is an expert on many things, which is why you pay to see her. But you're also an expert. An expert on your own life, on your spirit, on your soul. See if you can strike a balance.

Changing my life really worked for me. I learned so much about what will and won't make me happy. Some of those things have helped other people, and I love helping people. It just feels good; like it's the right thing to do.

I also have this burning lifelong passion for writing. And, voila, it all comes together.

If you want to read more of my work, check out my other book:

The World Is Better Than You Think—
Developing an Eye for the Good Around You.

Reading it is sure to increase your happiness. So you can determine if you might like it, I've included an excerpt at the end.

You can find even more of my writing on my blog:
inkshots.org.

I've included a sample after the book excerpt.

Then there's my website where you can read about all sorts of other things, like my divine guidance life coaching and tarot reading:
indiaholden.com

You can find me on Facebook by my full name:
India Susanne Holden
On twitter it's: indiaholden

Saying goodbye is hard to do sometimes!
If you'd like to drop me a line, write to:
india@indiaholden.com

Then there's my mailing list!
Go to: http://eepurl.com/cnncxX

Or scan this QR code with the scanner app
on your smartphone:

Be among the first to hear when I publish something new, throw a party, or whatnot. I won't sell your email address, share it, or spam you. Ever.

YOU CAN HELP SPREAD THE MESSAGE IN THIS BOOK

 Handy-Dandy
Spread-The-Word List

- Tell your family and friends about Crafting a Happy Life
- Leave a review on Amazon
- Visit my blog and leave comments
- Share posts you liked through email and/or on your social media
- Link back to my website or blog
- Post to my Facebook page about how you're crafting your happy life
- Host me at an event such as a
  -Keynote about Crafting A Happy Life
  -Book reading & signing
  -Crafting a Happy Life workshop
  -Divine Guidance Golden Tarot group reading

~ AFTERWORD ~

So now that you are well and away, I've got to tell you real quick that I love you so much. To be honest, I can't be sure that we'd like each other if we met in person. But seeing you in my heart, I'm mad-dash crazy for you. I would give you all my gold stars and poetry pictures if that were an option right now. Maybe if we see each other sometime, I'll have some in my pocket.

~ ACKNOWLEDGEMENTS ~

Even though you're the one who does the writing, you never write alone. There is the invisible support of your spouse, letting you work uninterrupted all day long and half the night, sneaking you the occasional plate of food and glass of water when you forget the time. There is the trust given you that you're doing your work and that your work has value. There are the countless conversations, the read-throughs, suggestions, thoughtful feedback, and encouragement. Others give you technical support to make your software behave (but especially the writer who operates said software). There are your friends who cheer you on with, "I can't wait to see it when it's done." Coffee shops and libraries provide a much needed change of scenery, though very hard seats. Technology pipes peaceful music right into your head, shutting out distractions and enhancing the mood. There are your four-footed friends always game for a belly rub and a good chat when you need time to mull a particular passage. I am blessed to be surrounded by goodwill, love, and delicious warmth as the weather turns cold. Fortified and comforted by chocolate, tea with milk, coffee, and the occasional small glass of scotch—got to be a little wild sometimes.

I want to thank Steven, my hubby, who, more than anyone else I know, deserves his nickname, *Angelman*. I want to thank my friend, the writer John Urbancik, who can always be counted on to help with the vexatiousness that is formatting and with any other writer-type question. I want to thank my mom(-in-law) whose love is a constant; it's plain where Steven gets it from. For their support, I want to thank Kayla Longaker for her encouragement, and helping to promote, Gaia Hawkin for her wisdom and for teaching me the tarot that broadened my connection with the divine. I want to thank the 2016 Gender Odyssey Conference in Seattle for creating a place where I could see my genderqueer self reflected: Though my gender journey isn't part of this book, spending time with

ACKNOWLEDGEMENTS

the rawest, most authentic group of people I've met has made me grow in unexpected ways, and helped me take self-acceptance and love for myself to new places. Those developments are expressed in how I write now. Lastly, I thank the divine: Your existence makes everything good. I love you so much!

~ABOUT THE AUTHOR~

India lives in Seattle with her spouse and their two dogs. India is a writer, speaker, certified life coach and Reiki master, and teacher. They (that's the singular "they," the pronoun India prefers) offer Divine Guidance life coaching, Divine Guidance tarot readings, and, when time allows, they instruct classes and workshops that teach many different healing and creation tools for fashioning a happy, meaningful, and joyful life.

"Long overdue - finally someone says it with intelligence and humor: THE WORLD IS BETTER THAN YOU THINK! This is not just wishful thinking. The author backs it all up with facts, research and well-rounded quotes. People always say 'I just want to be happy'! This book goes a long way in that."

"This book has confirmed some of what I already believe. If one person is kind or considerate (or realizes that others are) it can carry that kindness on to the next. I am already following some of the program. It's amazing how much more I now notice."

"With this book... you'll gain a more realistic perspective of all the good things that are happening right under our very noses... The result of the practices this book recommends is a more realistic and appreciative perspective on life that doesn't ignore the "bad," but helps you bring more "good" into the picture so your view of life and the world you live is better balanced.

[The] advice is straightforward, practical, and charmingly delivered...a quick read, but it isn't fluff – [India] cites some of the science...Spend a couple of hours...and you'll feel better. And then invest some time in the practices she recommends. You won't regret it."

What makes the world go round each day are uncountable interactions
conducted in good faith, with honesty and integrity, and often with love.

THE WORLD
IS BETTER THAN
YOU THINK, BOOK 1

Developing An Eye For
The Good Around You

by India Susanne Holden

INCLUDES THE 21-DAY PROGRAM, 7 STEPS TO NOTICING GOOD

THE WORLD IS BETTER THAN YOU THINK

~ EXCERPT ~

The world is better than we think. How could that be? Maybe it's because we're not in the habit of noticing all the good around us to give us that impression. But it's there. Trust me, I see it every day.

Up close and personal experiences with goodness made me want to write this book. For example, my life was saved twice. Literally. And by the same woman! She was a complete stranger who rushed out of her house to assist me after seeing me get hit by a car. The second time, four years later, when I was twelve, she happened to be there again. This time, I lost control of my beautiful blue bike while trying to jump the curb onto the sidewalk. As my tires slid into the street, she grabbed me and pulled me out of the way just in time before the city bus roared past. Without her care and attention, I'd be dead meat instead of writing this book.

But most often, goodness happens in more ordinary ways. This book gives you examples of human kindness and goodness. According to the U.S. Bureau of Labor Statistics, over 60 million people in the United States volunteered in 2014. That's roughly twenty-five percent of the population; you are likely one of them.

And rich people (yes, rich people) are taking part, as well. Bill Gates, for example. Some years back, he started the Giving Pledge. By now, over a hundred of the richest people have pledged 90% or more of their wealth to good causes.

In the last section of this book, I'll guide you through 7 steps in a 21-day program to hone your skills of awareness. Soon, the world will give up its charms to you.

Now, to be honest, I'm a lover *and* a cynic. Over time, I've learned how to let these two attitudes exist side by side. Like you, I'm well aware of all the mischief going on in the world, but we shouldn't let that stop us from loving life, from loving each other.

Every day, all over the world, we conduct ourselves with honor and integrity, and often with love (60 million acts of them in 2014 alone). From giving proper change to holding the elevator, from raising the minimum wage to treating chickens more humanely, we show our goodness. That's the grease that keeps the world spinning on its axis.

Each of us can take an active part in this, too. When we notice how good the world really is, we become change agents. Simply because it's a natural impulse to "pay it forward." When we do, we make the world even better than it already was. Are you ready for proof? Then read on.

NOW AVAILABLE ONLINE IN EBOOK FORMAT

You can read it on any device that lets you download a reader app.

Search by title:
The World Is Better Thank You Think

Or visit:

THE WORLD IS BETTER THAN YOU THINK.COM

READ ON ANY DEVICE

E-READERS   LAPTOPS
SMARTPHONE   DESKTOPS
TABLETS

SPOTTING THE DIVINE
AT THE BAR COUNTER AT
1:00 IN THE AFTERNOON

You know how, when you sit down at a bar, you can just never tell whom you might meet there? Often it's people who sit very upright and stoic on their stools though they're very drunk. Sometimes it's philosophers; or hopeful romantics.

As I sit down, waiting to pay my lunch tab, a man shouts to the bartender.

"I'll pay for that *and* a drink, if the lady will have one."

Against the impulse to shut him out, I say yes. He buys me a whiskey and calls me a beautiful woman. I don't have the heart to say, "Not exactly. I'm genderqueer." Instead, I say:

"I'll be sure to tell my husband you said that. He'll be tickled."

He is a drunk with advanced skills. With a well-practiced tongue, he pushes vowels and consonants around what seem to be marbles in his mouth. The thought occurs to me, 'I could *see* him instead of judging him.' I look into his eyes. They are enlarged by thick glasses and so open, so drunkenly unguarded and hopeful.

He just got back, he confides to me, from a damp, green North far away. He traced his ancestral line across two seas, stopped in Fiji and played golf in the warm rain.

He sums up his story, saying, "I love people. I have a beautiful life."

His eyes are moist with alcohol and feeling.

I think to myself, 'That love is your essence. I see you.'

We continue our conversation. He's just returned from Europe; I am from the Old World. He's been to Munich; I grew up there. We both love Paris; we drink to the City of Light. He talks about the money he's made and his daughter to whom he's close; I talk about a book I've written and about my work as a Divine Guidance life coach and tarot reader.

"That's a wonderful profession," he says.

We share our stories of becoming whiskey lovers. We even talk politics—he's Republican, I'm Democrat.

Unexpectedly, I love him. The shiny rims of his glasses frame his soul. I think of the famous exhortation, *Love thy neighbor as thyself.* For the first time, I notice that this pronouncement entreats the listener to love "themselves."

I think, 'Why not love this stranger by seeing him

as he hopes to be seen?'

I'm suddenly grateful that I learned to love myself over the years and can use this feeling as a guide to loving my boozy bar neighbor.

I am reminded of an exquisitely captivating book I read decades ago, *That Man is You*, by Louis Evely, that describes how to recognize Jesus in everyone. I notice how lovely my conversation partner is, the sensitive curve of his upper lip, the soft, yet dignified line of his jaw, the lightly tanned skin, the waves of graying blond hair. We raise our glasses and smile. I finish my drink. We say goodbye. As I walk to the door he calls after me, "My name is…" He spells each letter of his last name with slow precision.

I'll remember you.

**

Well my friend, that's the end of this week's *Inkshot*. I hope it gave you something interesting to ponder. Salute and may you have a beautiful, beautiful day or night, as the case may be.

Author's Note: This blog is a way for me to share my

experiences of the world being better than we think and moments of crafting a happy life.

More at: inkshots.org

DivineSeed
Publishing

~ HOW DIVINE SEED PUBLISHING CAME TO BE ~

In a *personification* session some years ago, I spoke with a part of myself I'd never met—what I decided to call the *Divine Seed*.

This aspect, unexpectedly woken, wanted nothing to do with this world. It only wanted to be home in the great ocean of divine oneness. I promised to dedicate myself to doing what I can to make this earthly life appealing to the divine seed so it would be happy to stay. Writing encouragements, such as this book, is part of that promise.

Awww. You kept reading. I love that. I do the same thing with books and movies. Sometimes there's another little tidbit and that's so much fun! So, here's one now: Thank you sweetheart, for taking this journey with me. I hope it does you a world of good!

Made in the USA
Middletown, DE
06 March 2018